SWING SHIFT

Peter Finch

Peter Finch

Copyright © 2018 Peter Finch

All rights reserved.

DEDICATION

This book is dedicated to all those who wish to improve

CONTENTS

1   Fundamentals

2   Backswing

3   Downswing

4   Through swing

5   Short game

6   Extras

Make your own notes here on what you learn and would like to look into more :)

More Notes :)

AN INTRODUCTION

There is no way around the fact golf is a very, very difficult sport. This novel idea dreamed up by presumably slightly mad Scots to propel a little circular object toward a tiny hole in the intermediate distance has caused immeasurable mental toil across the intervening centuries.

Its difficulty is not lost on beginner, regular or elite golfers who all struggle with golf's never ending challenges. For many golfers (mostly the ones reading these words) improvement becomes an obsession, trying to figure out why such a seemingly simple task can be so hard to accomplish.

Even non-obsessive golfers feel the need to improve, to strive for that sweetly struck iron or putt, to dream of splitting the fairway on their 'problem' hole.

This is why golf, despite the never ending heartache, is our greatest sport. An individual's strive towards improving in a game which can never be, because of its complex nature, conquered.

As a coach I see this striving everyday in person, on the driving range, course or by correspondence across social media. Everyone knows they must practice to improve, that is a simple statement of fact. However, the amount of golfers right now expending buckets of sweat and tears smashing balls at a driving range and NOT improving is beyond count.

I'm extremely fortunate to have golfers travel long distances to the Quest Golf Academy for lessons. The power of social media still astounds me and I feel very privileged to be in this position which has allowed me to pursue many of my ambitions as a golf professional. One of these has been to write a book and, well, here it is! The first of what I hope can be a series inspired by and dedicated to those who come to see me.

The SwingQuest series of videos on my YouTube channel (www.youtube.com/PeterFinchGolf) is based on improvements made by my clients and I hope in this book to expand on those sessions for the benefit of all golfers. Everything in this book is based on coaching carried out at the Academy and is therefore 'battle tested' during lessons and with feedback once my clients leave Quest and head out on their own.

This book is 1000% not intended to replace the need for individual coaching but to supplement it and help expand your current knowledge. I know from personal experience that whilst online video instruction and literature can improve a golfer nothing compares to one on one expert tuition. The player/coach dynamic can dramatically improve the speed of learning and advancement of performance and is well worth trying if you haven't before.

The lessons and coaching advice in this book is mostly based on the full swing, this is the area of technique where I spend most of my time although there will be more conclusive short game and putting books landing in the future.

It is my hope that by learning from people who have experienced lessons at the Quest Golf Academy you can become a better golfer and turn those tear soaked practice sessions into moments of real improvement, enabling better performance where it counts…the golf course.

A Note On Practice And Expectation

Most established golfers know the feeling of going to the driving range around work and family commitments, sometimes awakening at dawn to practice, others into dark reaches of the night. All with the goal of playing well in the weekend medal, taking some cash from friends, or just beating a personal goal.

After all the effort and expense, you stand there on the first tee, water beckoning the slice you've tried to fix the previous month by beating 500 balls. You take a deep breath and focus on the Rory like swing you've practiced………..whack, SLICE!!!! "Oh Dave, you've killed a bloody duck!" Tears, sometimes literal tears, can flow.

When working on a movement, any movement, practice is vital to improve. Your brain begins to form neural networks which allows the body to understand how it should react in a certain situation. You've already worked on forming these networks throughout a lifetime of repetitive practice and repeat them subconsciously.

Tying a shoe lace or brushing your teeth, you could perform these complex tasks easily with your eyes shut. This is because when you desire to preform an action your brain accesses the correct series of networks and hey presto! Clean teeth.

Golf works in the same way, a highly complex action which requires multiple simultaneous movements to function in harmony. The very best golfers in the world have honed these multiple movements, ingrained them, and now move for the most part subconsciously.

Supercharging a practice session so new movements are reinforced by stronger networks which allow you to think less when on the golf course is our goal.

But it will take time and effort. This is not a book of quick fixes and nothing can replace hard work.

A Note On Fitness

When trying to make changes to the swing, you are attempting to move the body in a new way. To make these changes easier, it helps if you are physically capable and fit. This doesn't mean becoming a body builder or Olympic gymnast, but having strength and flexibility will undoubtably help players in their own Swing Quest.

This book is not one about fitness but I HIGHLY recommend seeing a personal trainer to see if you have any physical limitations.

For many people this may feel like overkill and an unnecessary tax on time. But if you have the time it will be worth the effort and if not then try to make some time. I've never heard anyone complain about being too healthy!

The difference between golf specific workouts and general strength conditioning is currently being debated at length between trainers and coaches. This is not my area of expertise however I would highly recommend golfers prioritise flexibility if they have limited time to work out.

A Note On Mental Preparation

This is something which we touch upon in the book however there can be no doubt that a strong mental approach is crucial in both the way you practice and play. My own research and study into this area is beginning to ramp up as elite performance is clearly linked to how well a golfer can think on the course.

Some Fundamental Points

Many clients coming into the Quest Academy are determined to make big changes to technique in an effort to improve. This is commendable and sometimes necessary, however golfers often skip to swing mechanics rather than checking their key fundamentals.

For example, many golfers struggling with hooks and slices will bash a gazillion balls trying to change their swing and yet completely overlook their grip, which may be causing the closed/open face at impact.

Sometimes this is understandable. Players feel like their "swing" is the issue and therefore must be changed. But changing a fundamental (grip, posture, aim, alignment, ball position) CAN ALTER A SWING WITHOUT MAKING ANY OTHER CHANGES.

This is vitally important to understand. When you change a fundamental, you are changing technique. I sometimes get the impression from golfers they feel that unless a sweeping swing change takes place they won't make a 'big enough' alteration to improve. Remember that golf is often a game of fine margins and a few degrees.

Quick note, this book is written in the language of RIGHT HANDED golfers, lefties just flip everything around you'll be all good :)

Now a quick glance round at great ball strikers will show that grips, postures, and swings in general come in all shapes and combinations. Dustin Johnson for example has a strong grip and bowed left wrist (everything here says the ball should move left, probably with a hook) and yet he fades the ball consistently. Jon Rahm, another big hitter, has a weak grip, also bows the left wrist and fades it, Webb Simpson draws the ball with a cupped left wrist. This list could continue with top players contradicting the perceived norms.

I'm not advocating a blanket coaching "textbook" method. However, if a player and coach cannot make compensations in the swing allowing for these differences in fundamentals, then altering those fundamentals may be the best way to improve things.

Remember for every DJ and Jim Furyk there are dozens of tour professionals with more orthodox fundamentals. The exceptions don't disprove the rule, they show that there are other alternatives. Again this is why working with a good coach individually is important, they may be able to see things that a book or video cannot.

THE GRIP

This is an area of technique I simultaneously love and hate to change! I love it because grip changes can completely alter ball flight and hate it because it completely alters the feelings a golfer has whilst hitting shots, which is not always a positive!

Grip changes are notoriously difficult but ultimately very rewarding when implemented correctly. This is because grip has a direct impact on face alignment and wrist movements (amongst other things) which in turn has a huge impact on shot direction.

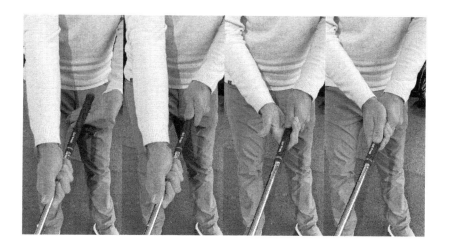

During lessons I've changed grips to neutral, strong and weak depending on an individual's needs. However most golfers would benefit from acquiring a neutral grip which allows the club face to move in a more orthodox way. But depending on your delivery (how the club arrives at impact) a slightly strong, weak, massively strong etc grip could be more useful.

I have listed here how golfers can acquire a neutral hold and the variations of the grip and what they could cause.

Neutral Grip

Named because of its ability to better keep the club face neutral (not closed, or open) to target during the swing, assuming the swing is also fairly neutral in its delivery. Take the club in the right hand and hold it with the shaft parallel to the ground at waist high, place the grip at the base of the little finger in the left hand. Leave a little room for the butt of the grip and make sure at this point the club's leading edge appears perpendicular to the ground. Run the grip through the fingers until it exits from the middle of the left index finger.

Wrap the left hand over and looking directly down (without tilting your head) you should see 2 to 3 knuckles*. The left thumb should be placed on top of the grip and not stretched down the handle, think short thumb. Then look at the leading edge of the club - it should still appear perpendicular to the ground. If it has twisted start again.

Place the right hand on the club, interlocked or overlapping with with left index finger**. The right hand then wraps over and the left thumb sits in the life line of the right hand. If these steps are followed correctly the 'V' created by the left thumb and forefinger should point towards the right chest whilst the right 'V' should point a little more towards the sternum.

*I've never particularly liked the 2 1/2 knuckle analogy, you either see a knuckle or you don't
**Overlapping or interlocking brings the hands together and melts them more effectively to the club. I generally don't see a ten finger or baseball grip being more beneficial, although I wouldn't be offended if anyone wanted to use this style.

We will now be looking at if you are a golfer with a weak or strong grip position. If you are unsure about which grip you have or how it affects your swing then this book will provide answers. But to be sure go see a good golf instructor and check out my YouTube channel for more information on how you may be altering your swing to accommodate a strong or weak grip. www.youtube.com/peterfinchgolf

Strong Grip

Named because of it's tendency to close the club face more during the swing and at impact

Using the same method as above move the left hand and right hand more to the right. This will bring the left hand on top of the club a little more and the right hand underneath. Strengthening the grip can help players (especially those who hit the ball right) to correct ball flight although it doesn't guarantee it. It also generally requires a faster body rotation amongst other things for effective delivery.

Weak Grip

Named because of it's tendency to open the club face more during the swing and impact

Using the same method as above, move the hands more to the left. This will bring the left hand more underneath the club and the right hand more on top. Generally golfers with

weaker grips will have more open club faces and less success achieving distance, exceptions include Jon Rahm and Jordan Spieth, although they both alter wrist angles.

QUEST LESSON EXAMPLE

It is far, FAR easier to correct a weak grip which causes a flailing shot off to the righthand side of the course than to alter a strong grip. There can be no doubt that a stronger grip feels more powerful which is why the majority of grip corrections unfortunately take this form. However, if a golfer has the courage and willingness to suffer short term discomfort the results can be awesome.

Whenever I look to change a strong grip in particular, I see what options I have because of the difficulty of this fundamental adjustment. These options were limited with John because of his launch monitor data and shot dispersion.

John had big misses travelling left of target and, with an inside path through impact, the first place to look was grip and hey presto! It was super strong. It's always tough to break the news of having to change a grip and I have the same formula.

"Changing this grip will feel very uncomfortable and it will take time to adjust, however this is what you can expect out of the other end".

Getting John to understand altering his grip would feel bad prepared him for the initial shock and I made it perfectly clear I wasn't expecting any good shots to begin with.

The carrot of what he could expect moving forward was enough to ensure inspiration, as well as heavy assurance from myself which was in constant supply.

Now it's pretty hard to predict how long a grip change could take to embed, but by the end of a lesson I hope to have a client pretty well accustomed so that their first practice session and round isn't a disaster (although this is possible - a grip which feels strange in a lesson can feel downright crazy on a golf course filled with danger).

However, John has a steely determination and by the end of that first session, he hit some incredible shots and tightened up the dispersion. Big changes are possible via the grip.

PRACTICE

Here's a funky little question for you, when does a practice session start? For most elite performers and golfers who improve quickly practice sessions begins before even arriving at the range or course.

Pre-Practice

Define your goal for the session.

This sounds slightly odd, the goal for the session is to get better, right? Nope, that's far too broad. Getting better is the ultimate intention but the goal for a practice session must be specific.

You must first assess what needs to be worked on. The most accurate way to do this is to keep statistics. Even the most simple stats will be beneficial but using a strokes gained* system is the best way.

Let's say for example your stats (or mental reckoning) show pitching from 50-100 yards is a real problem. This is where you begin to build a practice session and select its 'content'.

Choosing The Content Of A Session

When deciding what content to use in a session follow this formula.

Problem identification (example - wedge play 50-100 yards) and preparation

Technical Change + Competition + Assessment x 2 + Randomisation = Result

The Formula

Now preparation for a practice session (especially by using this book) will only take ten minutes but the positive results will more than make up for the extra investment of time. First of all, what equipment do you need? If pitching improvement is really the goal of the session, then take all other clubs out of your bag, you only need the wedges. Understanding the technical change you want to make is vital as this will form the basis for any block practice undertaken. Block practice means rehearsing the same skill until the feelings seem a little more natural (this is how most golfers practice all the time).

Competition or randomisation within a practice session is something not many golfers strive for; feeling more comfortable working through block practice is very seductive. However, using competition and randomised practice will help you improve faster.

Once the technique has been improved and competitive practice undertaken, a golfer then needs to take an assessment of the session before repeating the process.

Noting down the result of practice sessions can help refine your game later on down the line.

This is something Francesco Molinari has done to incredible effect throughout his career, noting down every result of every practice session.

Other Notes On Effective Practice

I always encourage people to practice as they would play. This means golf shoes are a must.

Always try to ensure you have a dynamic stretching routine and try, if possible, to also stay fit and healthy by working out. The less obvious reason for this is because research has shown exercise helps increase the production on myelin in the brain and spine. Myelin is a fatty white substance surrounding axons of some nerve cells. This layer forms an electrically insulating layer. Research has shown myelin allows electrical impulses to transmit more efficiently along nerve cells helping people (and in this case golfers) have more control over movements.

Having a good driving range, practice green, chipping green and course will be beneficial but not vital. Imagination and commitment is more important than a perfect driving range.

Some of the drills outlined in this book also require some extra equipment. For example a good quality phone and tripod to record your technique, alignment sticks and some other training aids.

Try not to practice on any one skill for more than 60 minutes. Even elite athletes struggle to maintain focus for longer than 60 minutes and I would recommend within an hour session incorporating a few five-minute breaks to refresh the brain. Remember the quality of your practice matters.

Before we go on let's have a look at how you can structure a practice session to help advance your learning in a particular area. Let's use grip as the example again.

EXAMPLE PRACTICE SESSION

Now perfecting a grip isn't overly complicated but boy can it feel funky!!! Even a tiny change in the grip and can throw a swing out of whack. However, repetition during range sessions will allow a golfer to grow more comfortable.

1. Technique Block Practice

Either by working on the above mentioned neutral grip or grip given from a coach, follow the process of holding the club out in front whilst placing the hands on the club. YOUR FIRST SHOTS during this phase of block practice should be with wedges and short irons.

I would recommend beginning with short chips and pitches working up to your 8-iron. After every single shot take your hands off the club and repeat. Try to have a specific target in mind when hitting shots, however in truth, to begin with, you may not get anywhere near it! But all feedback is useful. This section of shots should last between 20-30 balls and take about 15 minutes.

2. Competition

Now we need to see how accurate that grip is under a little pressure. Find two targets at short distances, ideally 50 and 100 yards. You want to be hitting five shots at each target.

In an ideal world this would be assessable. For example the target at 50 yards would be a defined green.

Whilst hitting these shots IT IS IMPORTANT to give yourself feedback and it will help you to see if the new grip is bedding in. Place a tripod (see equipment list at back of book for recommended tripods) and your phone directly face on in the bay. Try not to place it at an angle as this would distort your view on the grip. The idea of using a camera is to assess if you are slipping back to an old grip technique.

Assessing the success of the shot will depend on what targets you are hitting towards, to use the above example hitting 3 out of 5 shots into a 50 yard green.
Although it would be difficult to accomplish, hitting at a variety of different 50 yard targets requiring you to alter aim would also be beneficial.

3. Repeat The Process

Follow the same format as above then try once more to improve upon the test scores

4. Randomise

Now the real tests and practice begin! The goal here is to fuse the practice and play elements of golf. You want to hit a shot with EVERY club in the bag to a different target on the range every time. Follow the format above in regards to placing the hands on the club (this has now become your pre-shot routine) Then hit toward your target. Mark down the results and include the type of strike and ball flight you encountered.

5. Result

Review your success in all areas of the session. How does the grip now feel? How did the test scores improve/not improve? What was the difference in ball flight and strike? Do you need to repeat the practice session? Normally with grip the answer is YES!!

If you are looking to experiment with different grip styles then try the above practice session with weaker/stronger grip variations and see what you find.

PLEASE READ THIS ON PRACTICE

I have absolutely no doubt that moving into the future I will write another book and release many more instructional videos based around effective practice. Whilst this book mostly deals with technique changes which need to be practiced and implemented, it does not delve too deeply into practice techniques.

However, it is very important to understand that just standing at a driving range beating balls working on things you read in this book WILL NOT WORK, more needs to be done.

The reason for this is block practice has no consequence and very rarely gives an accurate account of what a golfer will face on the golf course.

Structuring a practice session correctly will help, however to be truly effective you will also need to practice on the golf course. The different lies you encounter, the conditions, the importance of making the shot at hand successful will help engrain changes much quicker.

A successful shot in a pressurised on course situation brought about by a swing change will help implement that change much faster than a two hour range session.

This is something I've proven during my videos using scramble tests to improve short game. Please visit my YouTube channel at www.youtube.com/peterfinchgolf to watch these videos.

The only issue you may have is if your course does not allow on course practice or you are not currently a member of a club. These are obviously impediments but find a way to overcome them. Once again practicing in pressurised situations is an absolute must for improvement.

AIM AND ALIGNMENT

Nothing, and I mean NOTHING is more overlooked than aim and alignment. It always amazes me how many golfers have very little idea where they are aiming and how that could affect a golf shot. The reason I find this so surprising is that golf, well…. it's a target sport!!
The lesson below is an absolute classic example of why aim and alignment are so important and shouldn't be overlooked. However, let me first lay out the terms we are dealing with and how my coaching relates to them.

Aim - I class aim as where the club face is pointing at address, throughout the swing and most importantly at impact. In my definition you aim the club and align the body around that aim.

Alignment - I class alignment as where the joints sit in relation to target line (ankles, knees, hips, shoulders). Conventional wisdom will have the body aligned parallel to target line - the line tracing from the ball to target.

If you are looking for a neutral swing in relation to target line then parallel alignment is a good starting point. Please be aware that alignment, or misalignment, of the body can impact swing mechanics and club data when using launch monitors.*

*Please understand that during lessons I have taught clients to align the body (or parts of the body) both closed and open to target to correct launch monitor data. Again individual coaching is very important.

QUEST LESSON EXAMPLE

When learning aim and alignment, it is always beneficial to head out onto the golf course. At a driving range, especially covered ones using mats to hit from, it is easy to become lulled into thinking you are aiming correctly when in fact you are simply aligning to the mat.

On the golf course with no such help from a range mat, true aim and alignment is brought into sharp focus. Nigel is a regular client I have worked with for the last few years and I am delighted with the progress he has made. Through intensive sessions and swing improvements we have turned Nigel into an incredibly consistent striker of the ball. His club delivery is super neutral with very little movement on the ball during flight. But there was a problem.

"Nigel, you are swinging it beautifully" (as another 8 iron landed on top of the previous shot) "How have you been playing on the course".

"Not great", Nigel would reply, "I just keep missing everything off to the right".

This was obviously vexing for Nigel, who understood how well he was swinging on the range but seemed unable to transfer this progress onto the course in friendly or competition play.

I knew something simple and fundamental must be wrong so we headed off onto the golf course on a cold grey wintery morning.

During playing lessons we always have a little match (get the competitive juices flowing) and I say nothing of technique for three to four holes ensuring I get a picture of what may have changed from the driving range to course.

The playing lesson took place at St Annes Old Links and on the first tee I saw the problem within possibly 0.02 of a second. Nigel was aligning his whole body 30 yards right. He then put the same wonderfully consistent action we'd developed at the driving range onto the ball. Smack! 30 yards right.

"There, there!" cried Nigel, "That's what I've been doing!"

Imagine the scenario. Nigel is frustrated for putting A GOOD SWING on the ball. His aim and alignment was causing the miss. I continued to watch the same pattern emerge over the next three holes. Right shot, right shot, right shot as consistent as anything you've seen. The only variation of this was a hook when the hands flipped the club face shut to compensate for the alignment.

Fixing Nigel was simply about executing a consistent pre-shot routine which allowed him to align his body better to target line, into a more parallel position.

The transformation was instant and incredibly gratifying (also slightly funny) as Nigel started to ping those lovely straight shots we'd seen on the range down the fairway and onto the green.

How To Align The Body With Pre-Shot Routine (Based On Parallel Alignment)

1. Pick out your target line - and in your mind from behind the ball, trace a line from the ball to the target.

2. Pick an intermediate point - spot something which sits on the target line usually 3/6ft away from the ball.

3. Aim the club face first - move into the side of the ball and aim the club face at the intermediate target (it's much easier to do this than aim at a far away target)

4. Align the body - pick a ball position relative to the club being used and stand with all the joints in parallel alignment to the target line.

5. To ensure you are aligned correctly use alignment sticks AFTER you have set up to the ball. This will give much better feedback.

Do You Need Parallel Alignment To Aim?

Just a quick note on aim and alignment. The above example with Nigel was simple because his swing is very neutral in it's delivery (very straight path, low point just after impact, face generally slightly closed to path causing draw/straight shots) but you can make big changes to ball flight by altering aim and alignment.

Changing body alignment can hugely impact path and angle of attack amongst other things, whilst altering club aim can obviously change direction. For Nigel (who has very neutral delivery) aiming him left or right would alter launch monitor data, swing moving further left or right. This would help Nigel shape the shot if he so wished. I won't go into this too much here, some of it is common sense, but again I would recommend seeing a coach to check your aim and alignment.

BALL POSITION

Ball position is a fun topic because of how it can fundamentally change impact for players. It's a topic which you can go very, very deep into because of what launch monitors have taught us about impact. Below we will look at a client whose ball position was causing changes to his swing. We will then look at best practices for different clubs.

QUEST LESSON EXAMPLE

Here we will have a look at Andy and the simple but effective change we made during his first lesson down at the Quest Golf Academy. Andy has been back in for further lessons since this initial session but getting back to

some basics around ball position and how that relates to the swing centre and low point made a big initial impact.

Andy started the lesson with a very wide stance on all his clubs but particularly his irons which made a consistent strike more difficult to come by. His short iron stance width was what I would typically like to see with a driver and his ball position was also a long way forward.

This is also a good time to discuss why using video is so important during lessons. Andy couldn't believe how wide his stance actually was. Using video allows a coach to show clients more easily where a change is necessary and the differences post change.

One big difference which was apparent after the change to a narrower stance and more central ball position was how little Andy was having to shift laterally during the downswing towards the target. The swing was much more "centred".

Stance Width And Ball Position

I coach ball position slightly differently to some in respects that I don't like to see it change with the irons in relation to "swing centre". The swing centre doesn't exist in reality but is the imaginary line running down the spine angle. I like to refer to the swing centre as the sternum or middle of the chest. This is more understandable for lessons when talking about ball position.

If a swing goes to plan (with the irons and fairway woods from the deck) the club will bottom out in it's arc just after the ball (low point), which is level with about the left armpit.*

For the short irons (wedge to 8 iron) I like to see the feet together at address facing the ball. Then I get the golfer to separate the feet, just a little step each way. This ensures the ball position is under the swing centre.

For the mid irons (7iron to 5iron) I get the golfer to start the same, both feet together with the same little step to the left. Then I like the golfer to take a slightly bigger step right.

For the longer irons the same process is taken with again a slightly bigger step right. With these steps you will also need to gradually edge further back from the ball accommodating the extra length of iron.

Using this method allows the right shoulder to dip a little lower which stops the angle of attack becoming too steep on the downswing with longer irons. It also allows a consistent low point to swing arc.

*This will normally manifest itself in a divot. I don't like to see a huge whopping beaver ripped from the fairway, more of a shallow sliver. You don't need to smash down on the ball to achieve a good strike.

POSTURE

This is both a difficult and simple fundamental to work on with lessons and I should be able to give you an insight into improving your own.'Good' posture however can vary massively from golfer to golfer, as we all have different body shapes, leg and arm lengths, flexibility, perception etc. Because of this I cannot offer a straightforward lesson example in this instance. But I can provide some guidelines to help you moving forward. As always, I recommend working with a coach to further your understanding of the posture.

When working on posture, I'm trying to achieve these things;

1. Room for the hands to operate
2. Body weight centred in between the feet.
3. An 'opportunity' for consistent delivery

1. Room for the hands to operate is simple enough. I'm looking for about a hand's width of room between the butt end of the grip and legs. To achieve this, start with the club held out parallel to the ground with the back upright and the biceps held gently into the side of the body. Keeping

the back straight* tilt over until the club touches the ground. Add a slight bounce and flex into the knees, don't bend them. Check the distance between the hands and legs.

2. With body weight (or mass) I want to see this centred right in the middle of feet, not towards the heels or toes. This becomes more difficult on sloping lies and adaptions need to be made accordingly. I won't be delving too much into body pressure here although we do use a force plate at Quest Golf Academy and there is a difference between weight and pressure.

3. Maintaining many of the angles created at address into impact can help deliver a consistent impact. There will be changes because of how the body will rotate but keeping the hips back and allowing the hands free passage through impact is very useful. This can be helped by correct execution of the posture, and the ability to maintain it.

*I recently heard a talk about how the diaphragm and pelvic floor can affect posture and the ability to rotate. In general, the research shows a straight spine angle is fine (many top professionals adopt this position), however having the rib cage a little more relaxed down can help with rotation during the backswing.

It does not take a golf coach to understand posture will need to be different for a 6ft 6" golfer with long arms compared to a 5ft 6" golfer with long legs.

However, there are a few key things I look for. Namely the hands hanging pretty straight down from the shoulders and the butt end of the club a hand width away from the legs. I like the knees to be flexed but not bent (more athletic than sitting) and body weight to be through the centre of the feet. How you find this posture is a case of trial and error, however the following routine should help.

Hold the club out at waist high, don't extend the arms out unnaturally, let them relax. Tilt over from the hips until the arms hang down from the shoulders. Flex the knees and feel where your body weight has shifted to, adjust into the centre of the feet.

PRACTICE SESSION

1. Technique Block Practice

For the technical block practice of the posture follow the routine outlined above. Moving up through the bag try and hit two shots with each club. You want to have similar sensations and try to adopt the same posture for all clubs. Remember the lie angle of the club alters as the clubs get longer in length (if you are using variable length irons as opposed to single length). So maintaining the same hand to body positioning is possible.

2. Competition

For the competition, pick out a short, mid, long iron and driver. You will be hitting five shots with each club. For better feedback on how successful the posture adaptions have been for each club, set-up a camera looking straight down your target line (see equipment page on how to correctly position the tripod and camera).

Find your target line and start hitting shots working up the bag. You are looking to execute the posture routine and make solid connection with the ball landing it as close to target line as possible. Make a note on where the balls have been going and what the contact was like.

3. Repeat The Process

This process of block practice and then competition practice will hone in your posture routine. The key is to not let tiredness creep in. You need to concentrate on every routine and competition shot. If you ever feel your mind slipping, take a few minutes to relax before getting back at it!!

4. Randomise

For this randomise test, work from opposite ends of the bag until you meet in the middle. For example start off by hitting a lob wedge, then move onto the driver, then the sand wedge, then the three wood etc. Posture can affect lots of different areas of technique but centre strikes are what we need here. Use some foot spray or impact tape on each club face between shots and note down where the impacts have occurred.

5. Result

You should be looking for a few things after this practice session. Firstly, how does the body feel? Practicing a new posture can be strenuous so adding in some stretching post practice is a good idea.

How does the new posture look from block practice compared to competitive practice? You should also look for consistency of repetition, were you easily able to adopt the posture by the final competitive practice element?

The backswing is one of the most practiced parts of the golf technique. One of the main reasons for this is how adaptable it can be. Because the backswing moves at a sedate pace when compared to the through swing golfers have more ability to control its movements.

There can be absolutely no doubt about its importance for many players who use the backswing as a way to prepare physically and technically for the downswing.

However, many golfers would benefit from thinking LESS about it. Remember the backswing just prepares you for a downswing and impact, you do not hit any shots with it. Look once more to your golfing heroes and great players across the decades, backswings come in all shapes and sizes.

THE TAKEAWAY

The takeaway is probably the easiest thing a golfer can control during the swing because of its relatively slow pace. This is handy because achieving certain things within this section of the swing can be very useful.

However, golfers sometimes attach too much importance onto the takeaway when having something serviceable can be just as effective.

Let's have a think about some of the best players and ball strikers currently on tour picked out for the way they take the club away from the ball.

Ryan Moore vs John Rahm, Dustin Johnson vs Jim Furyk, Rory McIlroy vs Rickie Fowler

This little mental (and during lessons video) slide show demonstrates huge contrasts in takeaway technique and reinforces the notion of having your perfect swing rather than a technically perfect one.

I'll only change a players takeaway if it could affect the swing as a whole. Sometimes changing another aspect of the backswing can alter the takeaway subconsciously. This is the best way to implement a change as often a player can improve the takeaway and not think about the remainder of the backswing.

That being said, let's have a look at the things I like to see in a takeaway which can, if executed properly, help achieve other good backswing movements.

Triangle - Connection - Width

These are my three pillars for a solid and simple takeaway.

The Triangle - when setting up to the ball the shoulders (with a line across them) and the two arms form a triangle shape. The triangle shape forms the basis of the second pillar.

Connection - Keeping the arms connected to the body (biceps touching the body but not forced inward), turn the triangle away. It's important to maintain the spine angle as you keep the triangle together.

Width   Keeping the arms connected, maintain the width of the club moving away from the ball. Don't let the arm move inwards. When viewed from down the line (camera placed in-between the hands and target) the club should sit in front of the hands.

QUEST LESSON EXAMPLE

Martin is a regular client and very good golfer. By the time of writing this, we are edging him towards a four handicap. I'm very proud of how he has improved during the last year.

Now Martin had what I will say is probably the most common issue I see with golfers and their takeaway. From the get go, he whipped the club very low and inside the body going back.

An inside takeaway itself isn't the end of the world but Martin's takeaway dragged the hands and arms behind the body. From there they stayed trapped behind, up to the top of the backswing. This usually caused a very trapped position during the downswing and big hooks and pushes.

We got Martin feeling the triangle moving and the body turning but exaggerated the feeling of keeping the club head OUTSIDE the hands moving back. This means that

at the completion of the takeaway, which I judge as when the club shaft reaches parallel to the ground, the club head felt very "outside" of a conventional position and an absolute country mile away from his old takeaway.
In truth when we watched the video, the club head sat directly in front of his hands when looking down target line. A classic example of feel vs real.

The results were instant and improved the overall technique, which is of course what we wanted. Remember there is no point changing something in the swing if there isn't a positive difference in ball flight and strike.

EXAGGERATION

The one thing I will not be able to emphasise enough in this book is how much a golfer may need to exaggerate a change to implement it into a technique. Using launch monitors, cameras and other capture technology in lessons is incredibly useful for this.

"I changed that soooooooo much", a lesson will say.
"Oh really", I reply, "Well let's have a look at the video. You felt like the change was huge, it was actually tiny, let's push it some more!"

The difficulty with changing a swing is that the brain has become accustomed to certain movement patterns, honed over hours of bashing balls. This means that to create a different swing you need to lay down new neutral networks and join together neurones in the brain. One way to break an old pattern is to introduce one which is completely alien but actually goes far enough to make a change.

QUEST LESSON EXAMPLE

Terry was struggling with an inconsistent strike and was producing some very funky launch monitor data. As he began to hit more and more shots it became clear he was over rotating his lower body during the backswing, over rotating the upper body also and leaning towards the target at the top of the swing. This grouped with a few other issues was creating a myriad of problems.

To combat this we introduced a training aid. Namely a lime green chair which sits in the academy. We placed it by his right hip as a blocker. The idea was to turn the right hip slightly and then feel like the chest was moving over the chair (tilting a long way from the target) and only swinging to about half way back, left arm parallel to the ground.

Now in reality if Terry would have achieved these positions a heavy, weak and short shot would have followed.
But of course the massive exaggeration pushed Terry just far enough to get him to where we wanted to be. A steadier

lower half, full shoulder turn and more orthodox spine angle. He couldn't believe that the video and his new swing were one and the same.

"That felt ridiculous", he said, "Like I was swinging to my right ankle with no turn."
Remember when making a change exaggerations may be required to turn a feeling into reality.

THE COMPLETE BACKSWING

Moving on from the takeaway are the series of movements which transport the club up to the top of the backswing. I will lay out some key points and how they are connected but a backswing is simply a means to an end.

Remember a perfect backswing is one in which a downswing is better positioned to succeed. You hit NOTHING with a backswing......well hopefully not anyway. The downswing is what really matters but a great backswing can help a great downswing become more likely.

WRIST HINGE

When and how much a player should hinge their wrists is a bit of a grey area. Some people prefer a fast hinge, others a late one. I sit squarely in the middle. By the time the hands reach shoulder high I want the wrists to be fully hinged roughly achieving a 90 angle between the left arm and shaft. This ensures the golfer only needs a little more body rotation to achieve an effective backswing.

With a neutral grip, I also like to see the back of the left wrist match up with the back of the left arm and cLub face. But if a player has certain characteristics within their grip and hinge, a slight, or even big, variation can also work.

Jordan Spieth for example has a relatively weak grip yet 'bows' the left wrist to compensate. Bowing the wrist helps to strengthen a club face position. Dustin Johnson has a strong grip and also bows the left wrist.....he fades the ball. He does this by some unreal movements through impact but it goes to show once again that a textbook model isn't always necessary, but remember the exceptions don't disprove the rule. There are also a large number of top professionals who maintain the left wrist, left arm, club face relationship and hit the ball just as well as Dustin and Jordan. They also do this with less compensations or adaptions, something we will look at now.

QUEST LESSON EXAMPLE

Ollie came in for a lesson at Quest Golf Academy struggling with a big hook mostly caused by grip issues which closed the face during the backswing. The club face being closed caused Ollie to drop the club behind the body and hit big raking hooks.

Now this was a classic case of Ollie compensating for a closed club face position by dropping the club inside trying to compensate a face with path.

This happens quite a lot and usually shows the golfer as having good perception of what is needed to find target. Ollie however was unable to consistently compensate for the closed club face. Therefore a change was necessary.

The grip change was tricky but the drill we worked on with Ollie was fantastically effective. We got Ollie swinging to shoulder high with the hands hinging the wrists and getting the club face matched to the left hand and arm. After checking these positions in a mirror we got Ollie to restart his swing and hit the ball. This pause drill was designed to allow Ollie to feel what a neutral club face delivery would feel like.

It worked and the downswing began to drop less inside as Ollie became consciously more aware the club face wasn't as closed, and therefore didn't need to make an exaggerated move.

One Of The Hardest Things NOT To Teach

This is an area where I continue to change and improve in my coaching and that is to STOP coaching a perfect swing model.

During my training as a PGA professional, my contemporaries and I were shown swing models (top touring pro's) and instructed to instruct our future clients in how to swing the club. These tour pro models were as you might expect; exemplars of technique. Tiger Woods, Ernie Els, Adam Scott etc. At the time, launch monitor technology had not really penetrated the coaching bays of instructors and if you gave lessons using video you were considered quite advanced in your approach. Not once were we told about coaching a player to swing their best swing.

The reasons for this were perfectly innocent and understandable. Get a client to swing it more like Tiger and they will score better. The prevailing wisdom was players like Jim Furyk and other funky swingers of the club were novelty acts, and rather than looking at the differences between golfers and seeing the variations of technique and how they can work, we were taught these variations should be eliminated.

This is one of the difficulties I've tried to overcome as a coach (and I'm not perfect), to try and help players change what they NEED to in a swing to become better and ignore quirks. I still use swing models during lessons but usually just to show how different players achieve their results. I never say "Lets get you swinging it like Ernie and copy his every move" but I may say "Your transition is fast leading to this issue, let's see how smooth Ernie is in transition".

This may seem an irrelevancy but it is crucial. You need to find the best swing for you, not the best swing for you to copy.

SHOULDER AND HIP TURN

Prepare yourself for some sweeping generalisations!!! The shoulder turn and hip turn are linked for every player to different degrees and can be tweaked to match.

For example someone struggling with upper body rotation during the backswing and with swing speed can squeeze out more power if the hips are freed to turn more. The opposite is also true, restricting hip turn will restrict upper body rotation, depending of course on flexibility levels. Now because of the natural tension being built up as the hips restrict against the shoulder rotation, there is an obvious correlation between flexibility and ability of the golfer to complete these movements. I highly recommend any golfer looking to improve golf specific fitness work, hard on flexibility - or as I like to say control over body movements without restriction (I do actually like to say that).

In general if a line connected the hips and a line connected the shoulders most golfers will benefit from the hips rotating 45 degrees and the shoulders 90 degrees relative to their start position. Now 45 degrees with the hips and 90 degrees with the shoulders is for visual reference, working with 3D body tracking systems such as K Vest shows good players very, very rarely swing to those precise angles. But I feel telling golfers to rotate 88 degrees coiling against a 38 degree pelvic rotation elicits a rather panicked look.

So the turns are very generalised in this description to simplify things not complicate them unnecessarily.

ARM POSITION

The Right and Left Arm

I think these explained in conjunction should make sense to people and the way I go about implementing them. Again, in this regard I personally like to see certain things at the top of a golf swing which I find give consistent results for many golfers. But once more having these factors present within a swing doesn't always mean a good impact, they could increase its likelihood however.

The Right Arm

Pretty simply, I like the right elbow to be pointing down at the ground and not escaping too far behind the body.

If you want me to get fancy, I want to right shoulder to be in external rotation. If the elbow is down at the ground and the right hand is moving further back (away from the ball) this is external rotation and is also very important for the downswing as we will see.

The Left Arm

I like the left arm to be along the same line as the shoulders at the top of the swing.

Again this image is based on what you can see with your own eyes in a mirror of preferably with camera in the correct position looking down target line.

The right arm pointing down allows a golfer to maintain control of the right shoulder and also makes moving the elbow down toward the ball (helping to shallow the club) a little easier.

The left arm being across the shoulder line helps ensure the right elbow stays more in front of the body whilst ensuring the arms don't become disconnected or "steep".
They are also linked in the sense that if the right elbow is down and not behind the body the left arm is easier to position across the shoulders and vice versa.

QUEST LESSON EXAMPLE

Gregor is a fine young golfer who has been coming to see me for a year now between his studies (he's also super smart). He's also a left hander! Which makes it possible to now switch around the arms (a silent left handed cheer echos across the internet).

Gregor's backswing was pretty good just a little out of control at times, the arms generally getting very high, wide and coupled with a huge turn could lead to awkward transitions into the downswing.

Now for Gregor, using the left elbow better (right elbow for you confused right handers) got Gregor to tighten up his backswing because the change also shortened the technique. This more compacted feeling increased consistency instantly and with hard work also allowed Gregor to start hitting fades, which he had always had an issue controlling.

Now we get to the fun part! The downswing is where things really, REALLY, begin to matter. It is with the downswing that the ball is sent towards (or away) from target. There are countless examples of golfers who make very strange movements during the backswing who can deliver a very consistent downswing and therefore ball flight.

It is however also the most difficult thing to change. Remember you will mover faster during the downswing at any other point. The faster you go the harder it is to control.

THE DOWNSWING TRANSITION

Many golf swings are won and lost during the transition phase. Very simply this is the point in which the backswing transforms into the downswing and the club begins its journey (some might say quest :)) back to the ball.

The whole golf swing can be both won and lost here, potentially good swings can become poor, and weird looking actions can become effective. The transition really does matter.

Because this is the golf swing there is no one correct way of doing anything! But we will talk about two very common factors that can help all golfers; sequencing and shallowing.

SEQUENCING

We will loopback onto the backswing here for a moment to talk about sequencing, or the kinetic sequence. When the club moves away from the ball, that motion is begun with the hands, the arms then move, the shoulders turn, the body rotates, and the right hip moves back.

This is a very simplified version of these movements and in reality, involves much more crossover between body parts, not to mention weight and pressure shifts. However for our purposes the simplified version will suffice.

When everything has been moved up to the top of the swing in this sequence, the reverse will be true moving into impact.

The first thing to move into the ball will be the feet, and body weight will shift into the left side (remember pressure and weight are different things). Generally, I like the feeling of moving into the left heel, which helps the hips clear a little more behind a golfer.

The hips will then turn, the body rotates, the shoulders begin to clear as the arms and hands reach the ball last into a perfect impact delivery.......HA! If only it was that easy! This is the fundamental movement pattern used by the best golfers in the world and can be worked on to create a smooth action.

To be a little self indulgent here and to answer a question many people ask on my videos, the above sequence is what I work on when trying to engrain a smooth swing rhythm. I take my time and try to feel this pattern in my body when hitting shots.

SHALLOWING

Now we have to get our definitions straight when talking about shallowing the club. For many people the thought process is dropping the HANDS behind the body during the downswing. For me shallowing is when the shaft drops lower than the backswing shaft plane.

I don't want the hands flying out and over from the top of the swing but dropping the hands in low behind the body whilst shallowing the shaft will create a "stuck" position. Couple into this observations of the very best players in the world, whose hand path is generally very similar moving away and up from address to down and towards

the ball during the downswing. Remember golf is often a game of opposites. If the hands move towards the ball with the right elbow pointing towards the ball, that club should be shallowing.

Now shallowing the club does not mean you will draw the ball. Shallowing can help create an in-to-out path for golfers but for me shallowing the club allows a golfer to then begin controlling the club face more with the body and not flipping the hands.

In simple terms if you can shallow the shaft down during the transition into the downswing, you can turn the body onto the ball, dragging the club out and around into impact.

Because this is such a key part of the technique we will talk about two lessons. One player who needed to shallow the club more and one a little less.
Both these examples also show how right elbow work in the backswing can help, I don't work on this with every lesson but I think these two examples crystallise things quite well.

QUEST LESSON EXAMPLE

Anthony came in for lessons with a very common issue. From the top of his swing the arms would move out, the club shaft becoming steeper than the backswing plane. From this point onward all he could do is adapt the posture and shaft in an attempt to make decent contact.

We started to improve Anthony's downswing by first adapting the backswing. By moving the right elbow inward we were able to control what the arms and right shoulder were doing moving down into the ball, and let gravity take control of the club head a little more.

The right elbow movement is difficult to achieve because of how strange it feels to the uninitiated. This is because as the body rotates around, keeping the elbow from following feels a little unnatural. However, using this drill it can become a little easier. I picked this up from PGA

Professional Dan Whittaker and it works as both a swing improver and body stretcher!

Take the left hand off the grip and tuck it behind the right elbow. As you turn up towards the top of the swing, use the left hand to hold the elbow steady and don't let it escape behind the body. Once this has been repeated a number of times use a wedge and half swing to mimic the feeling with both hands on the grip.

It is always useful to start with shorter more controlled swings when making a change simply because they are slower and more controllable, allowing a change to sink in a little faster.

That is the process we followed with Anthony and we started to see big improvements to how the shaft was moving into the downswing enabling a better turn and delivery.

QUEST LESSON EXAMPLE

Many people hitting big slices might look at someone shallowing the club with envious eyes! However, it can cause issues and wild ball flights. In this instance we will look at Maddie, who was shallowing the club and dropping it a long way behind the body moving down.

Again we focused initially at controlling the right elbow and shoulder and feeling like Maddie was playing a fade. This was a new feeling for Maddie who has never been able to play a consistent left to right ball flight before.

This is where individual coaching becomes important and exaggerating moves essential. Maddie had engrained this big inside position so feeling a new right elbow and fade feeling was tantamount asking her to slice it! However Maddie feeling like she could fade the ball actually produced.....a dead straight ball flight with downward AOA (angle of attack), and for the first time some divots!

IMPACT

A good impact (and golf swing) should be determined by the shot's success. So if you are reading this with a funky impact position but the ball flies where you want it to...

then awesome! If you ARE reading this however I'm guessing something is amiss.

Impact is where all my coaching begins and my thought process is as follows:

Where is the ball going?
Does it have curvature?
Was the strike centred, toe, or heel biased?
Was it a fat, thin, or clean strike?

Using the launch monitors FIRST enables me to gather data in an unbiased way. If you jump straight onto video swing "faults" will leap from the screen. Launch monitor data doesn't care what a swing looks like, it just tells you what happens at impact.

After these initial questions and consulting the launch data I then ask the following questions:

What happens to club face and head during the swing?
Where is the player aiming?
How does that correspond to alignment?

Look at the chain of thinking here because I think it's important to understand.

1. Begin at impact
2. Ball flight
3. Strike
4. Fundamentals
5. Swing

The last thing to change is the swing as altering fundamentals can change the swing and in this case impact, without altering anything else.

Please bare this in mind as I talk through the swing characteristics I like to see moving into, and at impact.

FOOTWORK

How the feet work from the top of the swing moving into impact can affect how other aspects of the swing operate. This means with good footwork the swing can become much easier. This surprises some people but it shouldn't! Remember your feet are your only connection with planet Earth during the swing, all your power and energy is drawn up from them, so yes, how they work is important.

QUEST LESSON EXAMPLE

Stephen is an eight handicapper who was struggling with a two way miss and strike inconsistency. A forbidding combination. It became clear when we began to analyse his technique that keeping better control of the lower body would be the key to delivering a more consistent impact. Stephen's issue centred around sliding the knees through impact. They moved down and inward towards the ball causing a pivot backward and a flip of the hands. To control this and to quieten down the leg and knee drive we introduced a handy little blocker drill.

A quick note on blocker drills. These are drills which put something in the way of a body movement or club head, hands, head etc. They are designed to give feedback. If the golfer moves in an undesired fashion the blocker will be

touched and a player will know if they have moved in an undesired manner.

Blocker drills can be very useful but be careful as these drills used incorrectly can also cause a player to make undesired alterations within a swing. Yet again, consultation with a coach is always recommended.

For Stephen we placed an alignment stick (hooked under a basket to keep it in position) running along his toe line suspended in midair just outside his right knee. This meant that if when coming through impact the knees slid forward the alignment stick would be hit by the knee and we'd have feedback.

We got Stephen moving his body weight onto the left heel not by sliding during the backswing but by rolling the right foot inward. By doing this he managed to roll onto the instep of the right foot and keep the right knee moving toward the target not the ball. This quietened down the whole lower half and increased the likelihood of Stephen being able to turn through impact and keep the hands passive.

This type of footwork is common with many great ball strikers, take the current Open Champion Francesco Molinari for example.

BODY ROTATION

Good body rotation through impact is needed to increase the amount of power a player can produce but also how much work the hands and arms need to do. Power and accuracy working in harmony.

Remember the golf swing is a cumulative result of lots of little things. Sometimes the little things are slightly, or a long way, removed from technical perfection but they work together. Jim Furyk is a classic example of lots of strange movements culminating in a consistent and repeatable impact pattern. Jim, or Mr 58, has excellent rotation by the way.

We know that the hips should be rotating but we also want the shoulders to clear. Some players have the shoulders square or slightly closed at impact whilst others are more open. I prefer my clients to shallow the club during the downswing and rotate the body hard through impact. This stops the club from becoming stuck and can help golfers manage the club face better. This is my preferred method as I've seen the most success with clients using this approach.

As mentioned some world class golfers, square or close the upper body. Very few however do not open their hips in relation to their address at impact.

QUEST LESSON EXAMPLE

We will look at long term client Andy now and I'm delighted about the progress he's made so far this year, slashing handicap and winning a few club comps. Andy is a good example for discussing turning and not sliding into impact.

This is something which often catches golfers out who have been told to "get into their left side" which too often culminates in a big hip slide towards target during the down swing. Now we want body mass moving forward and many great players have a lateral movement during the down swing but very few "slide". If a player slides, the left hip moves so much toward target that a golfer has to lean the body backward (tilt the spine away more) and flick the ball into the air. This lean back also makes rotating through the ball very difficult.

We also used a blocker during Andy's lesson to stop a slide during the backswing and through swing. This blocker is incredibly useful and gives fantastic feedback to golfers. I placed a chair (I use a chair in the academy but anything that sits around hip high is fine) a hands width outside the left hip at setup.

Then during the downswing asked Andy to move the weight into the left heel and turn the left hip back and out of the way. The goal is to clear the left side and not hit the chair. If you can achieve these two things you will have transferred the weight effectively and rotated without pivoting back. To test these movements fully golfers can use a force plate which measures where a golfer is moving their pressure during a swing.

Passive Hands

Something that perennially hurts and frustrates golfers is "flicking" at impact. Flicking is when the club head over takes the hands during the downswing and alters the swing's low point leading to fat strikes, thin strikes, clean and high shots. The reason this is important is that an inconsistent low point makes it very difficult to control AOA.

Now shallowing, and not sliding are two important factors which help a golfer not to flick, for example having a big hip slide into the ball can encourage a flick. So having other factors present in the downswing is useful before moving onto this.

QUEST LESSON EXAMPLE

David was a perpetual non rotator and flicker of the ball coming through impact. During the downswing, David's lower body stopped rotating and the upper body remained closed (pointing right of target) through impact. To correct this, David flicked the club at the ball to help get it up and away towards target.

During the second lesson, after some fundamental changes during the first, we used a pitching drill to help David get the new sensation of moving through the ball by rotating, not stalling and flicking.

The drill involves putting an alignment stick down the end of a grip into the shaft. If when hitting shots David flipped excessively, the alignment stick would speed up and hit

David (lightly because of the swing length) in the side. The point of this drill is to keep the alignment stick away from the left hip and rotate through impact instead of stopping.

The improvement to David's impact was awesome but stopping a flip at impact takes time and patience. A word of warning whilst using this drill: it is entirely possible for a golfer to avoid hitting the left hip by violently shoving the hands way forward at impact. Ideally on wedge and iron shots, forward shaft lean will be present. However if the hands are leaning excessively toward the target, you will de-loft the club and potentially increase AOA too much.

THE RIGHT SHOULDER

The right shoulder plays an under appreciated role in the eyes of many golfers. This is because it's not a position that many golfers understand or know how to adapt.

I'm not a stickler for insisting players adopt certain positions or swing mechanics. My first role is to improve impact and that can be achieved in a number of different ways. However the right shoulder is something which I pay close attention to as controlling its movements (and that of the right elbow) can help golfers with any number of afflictions.

In my experience golfers who have their right shoulder working in external rotation during the backswing are better able to shallow the club and turn efficiently. The right shoulder during the golf backswing will rotate internally or externally (and anywhere in between) and to understand the feeling you can use a very simple drill. Stand

upright with the right arm bent and the right fingers pointing towards the sky. Then move the right arm so the palm now faces the ground. This is your shoulder internally rotating. Then move the hand back so again the fingers point towards the sky. This is your shoulder externally rotating.

Many of the world's best players have external rotation of the shoulder during the backswing. It can be quite hard for the brain to understand 'externally rotate the shoulder' so the easiest way to change this part of technique is to focus on the trail arm. In many instances the right elbow will move away from the body during the backswing and enter internal rotation. This usually manifests itself in a 'flying elbow', but not always and I will offer a wonderful contraction after my lesson example.

QUEST LESSON EXAMPLE

James was suffering from a classic (and extremely common) issue of having the right shoulder in internal rotation at the top of the swing.

The reason this is an issue for many players is that as the shoulder rotates internally on the backswing, it is likely to remain that way during the transition into the downswing. This was leading James (as it does with many other golfers) to steepen the shaft during the downswing before early extending with the hips, and lifting the shaft angle to compensate.

We got James to use two drills which articulate the feeling required. One is very much an exaggeration and stretch of the required muscles. The other a mental image of what the golfer wants to achieve.

The first drill requires a player to set up as normal as though they are about to strike a shot. Then taking the left hand off the club wrap it around the back of the right elbow.

Turn away from the ball as though taking a full backswing. As the body turns back the left hand pushes the right elbow in front of the right chest into external rotation. This drill stretches the muscles along the back of the right elbow, arm and shoulder. It really works to hammer home the feeling.

The second drill again requires just a one armed swing to begin with. Holding the club in the right hand swing up and maintain posture.

Move the right arm into a position which would allow you to carry a plate (like a waiter). This will move the trail arm into external rotation.

James had a long lesson to try and stop his steep downswing and big right misses. By the end of the session we saw some huge changes and much shallower downswings.

A Contradiction!

Now, the right elbow undoubtably plays an important role in changing the rotation of the right shoulder but there are notable examples of golfers who internally rotate the trail arm and move the elbow a long way from the body (Jack Nicklaus). One big advantage of moving the right elbow up and away centres around the possibility of increasing speed by adding width. Players who do this usually have notable differences in the way they change the direction of right shoulder rotation during the downswing and power through the ball with huge body rotations. Again I'm not advocating strapping every right elbow down however for many golfers a trail arm in control and shoulder in external rotation will help improve consistency.

ANGLE OF ATTACK

One difficulty many golfers face is the ability to achieve a descending blow onto the ball with the irons. It's not as simple as just "hitting down" on the ball and a player can make a ball first then turf impact more achievable by working on other swing movements mentioned in this book. Remember the more a golfer hits down or up will change swing direction. This lesson and drill does not delve into that too deeply but here is an outline of how AOA changes swing direction.

We are going to be talking about 'D Plane' which might get a little heavy but try to stay with me because understanding impact will help explain some of the ball flights you might be seeing on the course. The D Plane is made up of the

direction of travel of the club and where the face is pointing at impact.

First of all, have you ever been to a golf tournament and looked at the divot patterns players create when hitting the ball arrow straight? They normally point to the left. When taking a divot effectively the shaft angle will lean toward the target at impact. If the club head trails the shaft and nothing funky is going on with the inclined plane of the shaft, then at impact the centre of the club (sweet spot) will be moving right of target line. You could a draw a shot from this position with a slightly closed face to path but open to target.

This is why if a plane base (think divot point) is moving left but a player is hitting down, their path at impact will actually be more neutral.

The same is true for hitting up on the ball. Low point of the swing could see the club travelling right but as the club moves upward on the inclined plane the sweet spot will travel more left.

I've included a link here to a very good video by James Leitz called - Understanding D Plane - it's very useful for any golf pervs out there. https://www.youtube.com/watch?v=rR2zLVBSQm4

For this lesson and drill I am assuming that the only thing you care about is hitting the ball first and then the turf and not about D Plane. So that's what I'll focus on.

QUEST LESSON EXAMPLE

A frustrating thing for many golfers is when they try to "lift the ball" into the air. This normally results in a golfer leaning back through impact and flicking at the ball. This was certainly the issue for David (another one :)) who had a very pronounced flick, causing the club to either catch the ball very cleanly, thin the ball or hit a fat. Taking a consistent divot was out of the question. He was the greenkeeper's favourite member, hardly ever disturbing the surface.

Flicking at impact can be caused by other issues earlier on in the swing. A big hip slide and getting ahead of the ball for example. However, David seemed just to fall into a similar flicking pattern approaching impact. One thing I noticed about David was his lack of rotation through impact. This is important because if a player rotates correctly, then applying shaft lean and not flicking

can become easier. If the body stalls then the hands can take over to deliver a literal flick of power.

We used a very simple yet effective drill with David to ensure he understood if he was flicking at the ball and not rotating.

We got David hitting some pitch shots and holding his finish with the arms extended in front of the body. The point of this was simple, if he looked at his arms and they had collapsed inward with the wrists broken down he would know instantly if the old movements had returned. This coupled with video feedback started to rewire David's movements.

How Deep Should A Divot Be?

There is no official text book for consistency of divot depth but you don't need to take big walloping mountains of fairway to hit good shots. A lovely sliver of turf would suffice nicely. And remember the D plane and what happens when you hit more up or down, swing direction will change.

Hitting Up On The Driver?

You can hit good shots striking down with the driver, players like Brooks Keopka and Dustin Johnson have shown this during the past few years. However, hitting up is generally preferable for a number of reasons. Firstly hitting down will generally reduce loft and as we all know there isn't a great deal of this to begin with. If we then add more loft, the downward angle of attack combined with more loft could add spin loft, causing high spin rates and robbing a golfer of potential distance.

Optimising launch conditions with a driver therefore often consists of hitting more up and from the inside. Players like Rory McIlroy do this amazingly well, as do many of the very best players in the world. Playing a round with angle of attack is something I would recommend every golfer to try. This drill revolves around swing centre and again, for this example think about sternum position.

Take a seven iron and place an alignment stick running from the ball through the centre of the feet. This will help a golfer identify ball position. On the first shot set the ball up from the very front of the stance (opposite the left heel) with the feet shoulder width apart. Try to keep the sternum behind the ball as you hit a few shots. You should find the ball launches high without much of an impact on the turf or mat.

Then switch the ball position to the back of the stance and keep the sternum position forward of the ball. The ball flight should come out much lower as the swing arc bottoms out after the ball. Little games like this with all your clubs should help you to understand how AOA can work in different situations. If you find this difficult, switch over to using a wedge and build up through the bag.

EARLY EXTENSION

Early extension is one of the most recent trends in golf coaching and has become much more understood during the last few years. Part of this is down to 3D systems which have been used to analyse the best golfers in the world and map certain similarities in movements they make.
This term groups in together the combinatorial movements which see the spine angle lifting away from the ball as the hips move towards it.

Generally the best players in the world will rotate the hips in a way which allows the original spine angle to be maintained and room to be maintained at impact for the arms to travel.
The rotation into impact can be affected by a number of factors including physical limitations (as can many movements in the golf swing) but there are some good drills which can be used to help maintain a good posture and rotation into impact.

Drill One

This drill will require a yoga ball and some room to swing but can really give a golfer an excellent feeling of what impact should feel like. Take up a golf posture pushing the ball into a wall with your backside. You want there to be enough pressure to ensure the ball wont fall when swinging slowly but not so much that the body weight falls into the heels. During the backswing feel the the right bum cheek move back a little into the ball completing a full shoulder turn. During the downswing keep the chest over the golf ball and rotate the left hip pushing the yoga ball back into the wall. If the yoga ball comes loose then the hips have move forward instead of back and around.

Drill Two

Place a chair or golf bag (or anything hip high really) just back and left from the left hip. Starting slowly with some pitching swings move through the ball and try to back the left hip into the chair. This will help ensure the left hip is moving back and left through impact.

Both these drills are FEEDBACK drills which will help tell the golfer if they are on the right track. If the yoga ball falls the hips have moved forward, if the chair isn't impacted it means the hips haven't moved through impact as intended. Feedback drills help ensure the golfer understands if they are making a different movement.

We are on the final furlong peeps! The through swing holds a duel distinction in my mind for not mattering at all whilst also mattering a great deal.

Firstly the through swing, which takes place after point of contact with the ball, has absolutely no effect on ball flight. Once the ball has been hit then that's it, you can no longer influence it's flight…unless you double hit it of course!
I see many golfers hold lovely long finishing positions which could have been carved from marble by Greek masters only to see their ball slice wildly off target. So one part of my brain says pre impact is what matters.

Another part of my brain however will chirp up and point out that changing something in a through swing can effect something earlier in the golf swing. For example changing a finish position can DIRECTLY impact how the club moves through the ball.
In my experience everything preceding impact is more important. Simply put getting everything working well prior to and through impact will cause a good through swing and that is my main focus. But there are occasions when switching up a through swing can have a big impact.

QUEST LESSON EXAMPLE

Keith had a rotation issue. For some reason he found it impossible to rotate the lower body from the top of the swing through impact. It was perplexing because he had no movement restrictions and his practice swings were much more fluid. Something in his brain was not allowing the body to turn and because of this his hands and arms dominated the the downswing causing a big over the top movement and topped shots.

You could see Keith found this very frustrating (who wouldn't?), because he understood what he needed to do but couldn't manage it. This is much more common that you might imagine. If the brain doesn't know how to relate the information, if the neural networks have not formed, the stronger connections will control any movement. The harder Keith tried to rotate and shallow the club the more over the top he came and less he rotated! To break this cycle we focused on two things.

I got him to make several practice swings where the belt buckle and centre of the chest would rotate together and made Keith feel they were fully rotated (facing the target) before the club had even reached the ball. This is a movement almost nobody makes but a big enough exaggeration to break his mental block.
Secondly I made Keith hold his finish position with his chest and belt buckle pointing left of target (for a right hander).

This is a deceptively simple drill but is essential because it helps a golfer feel but also visualise a change

With these huge movements I encouraged him to not worry about impact at all! Focus on turns and a super rotated and balanced finish position.

If I remember correctly he completely missed his first few shots, not even close to making contact. This is always a hard position for a coach. Making changes and seeing worse results initially is difficult but if you frame the situation and make a lesson understand that these feelings are so raw that you don't expect them to hit any good shots to begin with, they relax and trust the process.

All of a sudden it flipped. From missing the ball, Keith produced an explosive and powerful draw, it blasted off the face. He even managed to hold his finish position, belt and chest left of target. He held that finish position for a long time. We both laughed and carried on grafting.

Other Points On The Through Swing

The through swing has just as many moving parts as the back and downswing so picking them all apart could take quite some time. I have condensed down some of the more important aspects players should be aware of.

Please be aware these are observations and general opinions not set in stone fundamentals that must be observed. Also many of these movements through the ball are dictated.

HAND PATH

The through swing hand path is closely linked to the ability of shallowing the club during the downswing. Many players try to extend the arms and hands down toward the target through impact, whereas the majority of great ball strikers allow the hands to exit (lower and left) during the through swing. Hands which travel very high during the through swing will often point to issues earlier in the swing.

RELEASE

Release is a pretty interesting topic because of how it's often misunderstood. This is something I certainly did not fully grasp as a young pro. Releasing the club, releasing the arms, rotating the forearms all these different wordings can encapsulate what many players imagine as the release.

Many people think releasing the club through impact is how you square up the face and it can serve a purpose doing this. However, a golfer who releases the club in order to square the face will have an unstable impact and rely much more on timing than they need to.

Allowing the arms to rotate over in the through swing should be simply viewed as releasing power and not squaring the face. It should also be thought as a natural movement not a forced rotation. In my early days as a coach from watching old videos and looking at swings from books I assumed that the release is what caused the face to square up through impact. Unfortunately I had fallen victim to misunderstanding the dynamics of impact.

I include this here so people understand that as a golfer and a coach you must always be willing to learn and be wrong. If you head out into the world willing to disprove YOUR OWN biases and understanding the thinking of others with differing opinions you'll grow as a coach and a person.

BODY TURNS

Most of the top players in the world will have their shoulder rotation lagging behind the hip rotation. In other words at impact the hips will be more turned than the shoulders towards the target. Some players get the shoulders and hips almost in line at impact, such as Francesco Molinari (and he hits it pretty well).

However, just after impact and before the club reaches parallel to the ground many great players will sync up these body turns. This is a great thing to practice and can help massively with rhythm. Again a great drill for this is a pitch drill, holding your finish after impact and seeing if your movements have been matched. Another good drill for this is a slow motion swing which will allow you to feel the correct movements.

RHYTHM AND SWING SPEED

Everyone wants to smash the ball a long way and everyone wants their swing to look like a smooth flowing chocolate waterfall. Not many golfers however manage to find the combination which allows power and control to work in harmony.

One of the things I hear many well meaning playing partners tell their friends is "slow the swing down". It's something I hear in lessons also, "I know I need to slow my swing down".

My answer is always why? Why would you slow down? All that will happen is the same funky technique at a slower speed. Imagine telling Brooks Koepka to slow down if he hits a dodgy one. Speed is a blessing. If you can generate it, maximise it.

Now for the counter point. How you generate the power matters, swinging fast is not just launching yourself at the ball. Swinging fast with a chocolate waterfall rhythm is about correct sequencing and a sound body. Often what players see as a fast swing is a transition from the backswing to downswing which works out of sequence.

Let's start this in reverse. Having strength and more importantly flexibility is vital. Flexibility is a key which unlocks greater control over body movements. If you are prioritising one over the other choose flexibility unless you have time for both.

So let's talk about sequencing. This simply put is the order in which the body will move during the swing. Some of these movements will allow the generation of power and a better rhythm.

During the takeaway, the first movement is with the hands away from the ball followed by the arms, shoulders, torso, then the hips begin to open which moves the knees and feet.

At the top of the swing the shoulders should have turned fully until the middle of the back faces the target line. The shoulders turn more than the hips, usually about twice as much. This generally equates to 90 degrees of shoulder rotation (if you think of the shoulders as one unit) and 45 degrees of hips rotation in relation to their starting point which I generally think of as parallel to the target line. During the downswing the sequence is reversed. First the feet draw energy upward by pushing pressure downward and left, then the legs, hips, and torso all rotate into the ball. The last thing come through are arms, hands and club. This is a good sequence to move the body.

This sequence combined with other movements already jotted down in this book will allow the opportunity to generate speed.

Just a quick note on the sequence mentioned above. This is simplified in a way to help a golfer understand the movements and think of them individually. Of course unless you isolate the joints, your hand, arm and body movements will work in harmony.

Now the question many people ask is when to apply power. Generally speaking after the club shallows and hips begin to turn, if the player works the transition well then they should be able to continue to turn as hard as possible through impact. Now there are other aspect to this such as angle of attack, swing direction and strike location which must be also correct to maximise ball speed.

As mentioned above many people rush the transition from the backswing into the downswing. This is usually in an effort to force power. However when golfers force anything it usually manifests in the the hands and arms throwing the club towards the ball. Ultimately this reduces the speed at impact because of compensations a golfers has to make.

QUEST LESSON EXAMPLE

When a lesson comes into the Quest Academy, distance is actually rarely mentioned as an area the client wants to improve. This is just a general observation but most golfers highlight "consistency" as something they need more of. Potentially they are trying to tell me (and themselves) what they think I want to hear or maybe they understand the true importance of accuracy for a handicap golfer.

Jon however had none of these musings on the subject. "I want to hit the ball further, I'm so short". He said this with a real resignation in his voice. "There is a ditch at my home club on the 5th hole, it's 200 yards to carry and my playing partners fly it easily. I'm stuck because I can't carry it and have to lay up with a fairway wood."

This is what I call a directly measurable goal. Jon wants to hit the ball further (as do most golfers, I've not had anyone come in and say they hit it too far!) and has a direct and immediately measurable target. To clear that ditch.
Now golfers seeking distance have two primary areas they need to improve, strike and speed. Strike is oddly overlooked here as finding the centre of the club face will help transfer power more effectively onto the ball. Your current club head speed may be adequate for whatever distance goals you have but be scuppered by a poor strike. Jon had pretty good smash factors for his iron and driver swings meaning the transfer of energy from swing to ball was good. His swing speed however was lower than it needed to be to clear that ditch.

With a driver Jon was generating in the mid 70mph speeds

which combined with a good strike, AOA, launch and spin rate could have just about carried 200 yards, but everything had to be present.

Now Jon is in his 50's and fairly mobile apart from some flexibility issues in his lower back and legs. Looking at his swing we could see quite clearly where the lack of speed was arising from.

Jon had a limited backswing turn, think 3/4 swing, which stemmed not from his shoulder turn but a lack of hip turn. This restricted how much he could rotate away from the ball, extend his arm swing and get width.

From this position he would throw his arms at the ball resulting in an over the top action and slash through impact. What is interesting about players who struggle with a smooth transition, because of rotational issues, they usually look like they are swinging fast whilst actually swinging slow. Notice the irony of a slow smooth looking fast swinger! Rory McIlroy is my favourite for this. For Jon we ensured his hips rotated correctly during the backswing which instantly helped ensure more shoulder rotation. This created the potential for faster swing speeds but didn't guarantee anything. Remember the backswing is just preparation for the through swing.

We then got Jon to shallow the club more during the transition by slowing this part of the swing down, before turning on the power with rotation.

Now I would love to say that Jon was cured instantly and was whopping his driver instantly however power generation and distance rarely comes that easily. However, two months and two lessons later. "I did it!! I managed to sail over the ditch with a driver today, I was so excited I hit some of the biggest drives I have for years!"

If you manage to move in a good sequence the swing rhythm should take care of itself. However a great way to envisage what rhythm you would like to see is visualising your favourite players swing and imitating it.

This sounds a bit silly but from personal experience using this drill does work. To indulge myself for a moment I often get asked about my swing rhythm and how I engrained it, it was with this drill.

In my case I imagined the swing of Colin Montgomerie over and over again. I imagined Colin's swing because I thought it matched my personality of relaxed and languid, I also generally play with a slight fade. This is still a drill I use to this day, although the swing I envisage is different, who could it be?

A Note On Equipment

Now, I must own up to a certain amount of hypocrisy here. I always tell my lessons that good equipment isn't absolutely essential for good golf. I know so many players using clubs from a decade ago playing off good handicaps and many golfers who buy a new driver every month and can't stop slicing it. The swing, the thing you move a club with, is obviously more important than a shiny new stick.

However, I love getting shiny new sticks!!! I'm not immune

to the lure of a new driver, irons etc when they are released. Manufacturers do a great job of enticing people with promises of better golf (usually more distance) and it works. For me putters are a particular weakness, it's not my fault I missed that three footer right?

But let's look at this logically. Golf club design during the last 10 years has been evolutionary not revolutionary, meaning a driver from 2010 can still be a pretty damn good club. Irons are even more likely to have less change in their design than drivers.

My main priority is that whatever clubs a player has, they are fitted correctly for a player's build (height, arm length etc). For many beginners getting the basic fit right is important so they don't develop complications down the line from using clubs which are too long/short for example.

If you are looking to get new clubs make the commitment to stick with them for a long period and get fitted by an expert.

SHORT GAME

As mentioned in the introduction this book looks mostly at the full swing and I will only touch upon the short game. This is not because I underestimate its value, in fact this couldn't be any further from the truth. However, the short game deserves a book on its own which I will look to complete in the not too distant future.

However what I will give you here are three short game skills tests which will help improve your touch and feel around the greens and on longer pitches. Two of these tests take place on the course whilst the other can be completed around a chipping green.

SCRAMBLE TESTS

These are an absolute game changer for golfers who use them and yet hardly anyone does! Scramble tests need to be completed on the course because of the variation they produce and the fact it will impact your score directly. Here are the rules.

Over nine holes you are going to test your short game to the max. First of all set a target score. As a pro I'm always looking to beat level par using this test but you can make it appropriate to your handicap level. In a best case scenario use the scramble test to set a benchmark score

1. Every green you hit in or over regulation you must throw the ball off the green and attempt to get up and down. You can randomise this anyway you wish (1st hole throw off the front, 2nd hole off the back etc) but don't avoid shots you are uncomfortable with and don't prefer your lie.

2. If you hit a green under regulation then proceed and play the hole as normal. For example hitting a par five in two or driving a par four. This is because the player wants to remain attacking and seize opportunities to convert birdies.

3. If you land within 50 yards of the pin in regulation then proceed as normal. This is already a test of short game so go ahead and score! For example driving it within 50 yards of the pin on a par four or within 50 yards of the pin on a par five approach shot. This doesn't apply on par 3's.

4. If you stiff an approach shot within a putter length then proceed as normal. This again promotes an attacking mindset especially on par 3s.

This test will see you hit a short game shot from a random location on every hole you don't play amazingly well.

Example Four Holes.

1st hole - par four - 420 yards

A good tee shot down the middle is followed up with a solid short iron second which finishes five yards from the pin. This is not within a club length however so I throw the ball off the front of the green. It rolls from the surface and onto the fairway approach. I don't get up and down and slip to +1

2nd hole - par five - 530 yards

I stonk a tee shot straight down the pipe and leave myself with a difficult fairway wood shot to attack the green in two or lay up to a safe area 100yards from the pin. I choose to attack and attempt to get the ball within 50 yards of the hole. I find a green side bunker but as I am close to the hole I can play on as normal. I hit an OK bunker shot but hole a cracker. Level par

3rd hole - par three - 180 yards

The pin is tight behind a bunker which I normally wouldn't take on but I know it must be stiff to avoid throwing the ball from the green. I bail out a little and find the green centre. I now have to throw the ball right off the green. A good up and down sees me stay at level.

4th hole - par four - 400 yards

Two average shots sees me miss my approach short left of the green. Because I've missed the green under regulation I play on as normal.

This is a game which puts pressure on the short game as long as you give yourself an appropriate target and really want to improve your short game.

50 Yard Tests

The 50 yard test is very simple and can be changed to any short game yardage you may be struggling with. Very simply, when walking up the a green playing a social or solo round, drop a ball down at 50 yards from the pin.

Proceed to hit your pitch shot and continue playing with both your original ball and 50 yard test ball. Keep a separate score card of the 50 yard tests, play them all as little par 3's, how low can you go? Again it may be useful initially to set a target to beat by setting a test score.

Station Spot Chipping Drill

Now if you are going to use one drill around a chipping green let it be this one! I use this drill mainly with clients and their wedges. I carry four wedges, therefore I set-up four stations when using this drill.

These stations are placed in different locations to the side of a chipping green. Preferably you will be hitting shots from each station to the same pin but with different lies. This is not always possible but will aid development in the long run.

At my four stations I place five balls. I first of all complete the drill with my 60 degree wedge. I do this by hitting a single shot at each station before moving to the next. My goal is to either hole the chip or leave the ball a club length from the cup (gimme range). If one or more of my chips finish outside this radius I return the ball to the station I missed from. This means I will have more shots from the stations I have difficulty with. You can move all the successful shots to the side of the green. I will complete the drill by clearing all my stations of balls! Then I will replace the five balls at each station moving onto a 54 degree wedge and completing the drill again.

This dill will help players understand the different flights they can expect from different lies and experiment with spin and run out. It also adds a pressure element because if the stations are not cleared then the player cannot move on.

This is a drill which can also be adapted for any number of short game shots from bump and runs to high floating flops.

PUTTING

Ahhhh putting :) Now this is quite literally a book on its own and therefore I won't hammer home any technical points which may have been covered elsewhere. Most of my coaching is made up of the full swing then short game. I very rarely coach putting and my knowledge in this area is not as extensive as the full swing. Therefore until I have that expertise I will give you some excellent drills which can help you improve on the putting green no matter your stroke type. These drills work and have been tested on numerous golfers, including me!

A Quick Note On Training Aids

I use a number of training aids for my own game and for lessons who wish to work on their putting. Most of these are from Visio, the training aid brand pioneered by putting coach to the tour stars Phil Kenyon.

Training aids are very useful and can help guide a technique to a desired outcome. However, I would always recommend getting a putting lesson to help steer your technique in the right direction. I personally use Lee Sullivan based at the Putting Solutions studio at Tour X near Wigan, UK.

The Spieth Test

I devised and completed this test a few years ago based on an interview with Jordan Spieth who at that time was the best putter in the world. He said on a non tournament week he would hit a thousand putts. Now I had no real concept of how much time this actually takes, but trust me it's a lot, a back breaking amount. So I have come up with a condensed Spieth Test which is still pretty arduous but wont cripple you.

To see this test punch into YouTube "The Spieth Test Peter Finch" and it will appear at the top of the search engine.

Some Drills

Block Practice

Block practice should be used to specifically work on technique. I use a Yes! putting plane board, this is an old training aid but it helps guide my stroke. I add a competitive element to my block practice usually forcing myself to hole a specific number of putts, 20 from 4 ft, in a row before I can move on. This type of practice is useful to work on technique but should not become your 'focus'. By this I mean you need to work on this enough so on the course you can go unconscious. In other words forget what you've been working on, focus on target and trust everything has been ingrained.

Targeting

Targeting is all about line and pace control, in other words everything you need to hole a putt. However targeting is fascinating because it forces a golfer to hole a 'perfect putt'.

This might sound a little odd but most people don't hit 'perfect putts'. By perfect I mean the exact line with the exact pace a golfer imagines. Targeting forces a player to perform a perfect putt by placing two objects on the green over a 20 ft putt.

The first thing a golfer needs to do is find a breaking putt which requires an aim outside the hole by at least a few feet. Place a marker to the side of the hole which you will be aiming at, call this the aim point. Then place a marker 2/3 distance from the hole over which the ball will begin to turn towards the hole. This is the break point. I use a Visio fake hole for this. The idea is to visualise the putt and imagine the actual hole just getting in the way of the ball which would finish just past the hole.

Area Putting

This drill is designed to work on speed from a desired distance. Set some tees out on the green in a semi-circle around the back of a hole, I usually set up mine to tap in range. The point of this is to hit putts you are trying to hole!! This is important, I don't believe in any dustbin lid type of thinking, when you have a putt visualise holing it not getting it close. If the putt misses however you want it finishing just past the hole within the small semi circle you have created. I normally do this with a maximum of five balls which need to finish in or just past the hole before moving on to another hole and distance.

Ladder Stations

Ladder stations is a variation on the ladder drills and involves setting up six stations ranging in distance moving back from the hole. On the first two stations a golfer needs to hole 3/3 putts before they can move on. These putts are normally 3 and 4 ft. On the next two stations they need to hole 2/3 from 5 and 6 ft before moving on and then 1/3 from 7 and 8ft from the hole. The pressure element is added in the form of not being able to move on from a set of two stations unless the number of putts holed is achieved. More pressure can be added by increasing the amount of putts which need to be holed.

A Further Note On Putting

On a personal note, I LOVE putting and the challenge it entails. Psychologically it's a true crystallisation of how sharp your thinking is and how much "bottle" you currently have, how much do you want to hole that putt! Courage on the putting green is something which can be learned, of that I'm 100% sure. Just like correct putting technique it can be learned and honed.

Put it this way, we have ALL been over a putt and changed our mind about which way it will break, made last minute adjustments and missed. On the surface this might seem like we are trying our hardest to hole the putt, in reality it shows non commitment and indecision.

Putting also offers golfers a unique opportunity. You might never be able to swing the club like Rory or DJ, that time could have passed. However, almost ANYONE could become a world class putter because it requires no explosive physical movements.

Shouldn't that excite you? Knowing that you CAN become an incredible putter even if you might not be able to carry it 300 through the air? Think on these words when next prioritising what to practice.

PRE-SHOT ROUTINE

Eight Step Bullet Proof Routine

Many people think they don't need a pre-shot routine or that it's too complicated however I can tell you now, you DO have a pre-shot routine. Humans, as the saying goes, are creatures of habit and these habits are formed very quickly. If you are inclined toward self experimentation you can film yourself on the course and notice you have the same tendencies before each shot, even if you don't think about them. It can be an interesting experiment I recommend you trying.

The quicker you can break a bad habit loop and introduce better processes, the better your golf will be, simple. Habits can be tough to break however, so this takes time and effort but it will be rewarded over a season.

1. Assess the Lie - Before you even decide what type of shot you are trying to hit check your lie. It's amazing how many times as golfers we make a decision on the shot we are going to play without assessing the lie. On many occasions the lie will dictate the type of shot you might be able to pull off. But if the ball is lying in the fairway or rough or sand or on a sloping lie, these will all influence how the ball will react when struck.

2. Conditions - Where is the wind direction, is it a warm or cold day? Is the ground wet or baked? Again play these things, and others, in your mind to come up with a better idea of how the shot will come out.

3. Target Location - Where is the pin? This is the first thing golfers need to assess on an approach shot and if that pin location is worth attacking. You will be amazed when watching the best players how often they hit AWAY from the pin. Target location also needs to assess fairways or landing points in exactly the same way. How is the fairway angled? Where are the bunkers and most importantly (certainly for players with better ball control) where is the pin? Will a shot from the left side of the fairway open up a green? Are you planning the hole from green back to tee.

4. Distance from the target - Now this again is pretty self explanatory...sort of! First of all most club competitions allow the use of a distance measuring device such as a laser or GPS. It is a luxury but if you have the means and play golf often I strongly recommend you get such a device. Now depending on where the target is will depend on the distance you need to hit. Remember your target is not always the pin, it could be the centre of the green.

5. Shot Selection - All the previous four points feed into this. What shot does the lie, conditions and target location allow you to hit? Process the info and come up with an answer, a clear and concise answer.

6. Practice Swings - Stages 6 and 7 can bleed into each other slightly but I like to take my practice swings before visualisation. The practice swings are designed to help get the body and mind ready for the shot you have selected to play.

7. Visualisation - This is one area where most golfers struggle, "seeing the shot". Like anything else in golf visualisation requires PRACTICE it's not something you will achieve suddenly. Have a range session where you just work on visualisation. You will be surprised at how exhausted you can become. A sign that this mental muscle needs more work. Visualisation works differently for different people. I see the shot taking off with a "shot tracer" style of flight. This is easy for me because of the amount of time I've spent editing such shots on my phone and laptop. But you might see it differently.

8. Execute the shot - After you've been through all of these steps. See it and hit it. Believe in the shot.

Remember that a pre-shot routine does not guarantee a good outcome. You can still execute a perfect routine and duff it. But consistently applying a routine over the course of a season will greatly enhance your chances of success. This is one of the huge differences between amateur and professional players, the consistency and positive features of a good pre-shot routine.

A Conclusions, Of Sorts

As mentioned earlier this is not a far reaching, deep dive into any specific area of the golf swing but more a general overview of things I've learnt whilst coaching at the Quest Academy.

For me being a coach is not about knowing everything, it's about the desire to learn more and pass that information on. No golf coach is perfect and knows everything, in fact you should actively mistrust anyone who claims such a thing. In golf there is always something new to learn and always another angle from which golfers see the game. For my part, I hope you can see I don't coach a particular method although there are some things I prefer to see in a swing, I try to coach the individual to produce the best movements they can.

I also hope that you have found in this book something useful which you can take away and learn from. Because this is the main reason being a coach is worthwhile, seeing people improve and reach their goals. What is your goal? Figuring that out can inspire you to keep moving forward. But remember, you will never beat golf. The game will always win. This is why you keep coming back, an unconquerable foe against which the war is ultimately lost, although battles can be won. It's also a game which tests your character and teaches you about your own nature, sometimes painfully, but always asking questions.

Lastly it's a game which gets you out walking amongst the trees at sunset, in a desert at dawn and on the beach at noon. A testing, trying, revealing, frustrating, exhilarating walk through nature, yes I love this game, I hope you can too.

Some Golf Related Thanks Yous

This book would quite literally not be possible without the amazing people who come and see me at Quest Golf Academy for lessons. It staggers me how far people are willing to travel for coaching and I am deeply humbled so many of you make the journey.

Coaching someone to achieve a goal is very rewarding but it also helps me connect to everyday golfers, hear their stories and learn more about this game.
So to those who have already been to see me, thank you, and to those making the trip in the future, thank you in advance.

There have been many people who have influenced my coaching techniques. Dan Whittaker who I regularly film with has helped to deepen my knowledge of how the body and club can move through the swing. Lee Sullivan at Putting Solutions has helped me understand the putting stroke much better but also taught me how to adapt coaching around a client.
And lastly to all my followers and subscribers across social media. As well as your support you have constantly challenged me to come up with new ideas and communicate my ideas better. This book is ultimately for you, those who can't physically get to me for coaching. Social media has allowed my to reach further than I ever thought possible, and who knows where it will lead me next.

39144022R00057

Printed in Great Britain
by Amazon